HOW TO WRITE A SONG ON A UKULELE

How to Write a Song on a Ukulele

RACHEL GARDNER

Cover Illustration by Bec Lynn

Treachery Publishing

First Printing, 2022

Contents

This book is dedicated to my two songwriting partners, Bec Lynn and Elizabeth Murray. Thank you for the inspiration, encouragement, suggestions and editing.

Special thanks to my boys Tavi and Kelson for their always honest feedback regarding songs that I write, and to Brian for the ongoing support for all the crazy adventures I ask him to partake in.

Chapter 1

Getting Started

So, you want to write a song. Whether you are an accomplished songwriter or just need a way to fill some time sitting at the park with your ukulele, this book is meant for anyone. Perhaps you can gather some tips and inspiration, or possibly learn from my mistakes. Songwriting, thankfully, doesn't have any rules, but if the lack of rules makes it hard for you to get started, how about some tips and tricks from someone who has stared at an empty page and found a way to turn that blank page into a song?

The first question to ask is, why do you want to write a song? There are no wrong answers, but the response you have can help guide the song you are writing. Is the song for someone in particular? Is it to perform in front of an audience? Is it to challenge your mind or to process an emotion? Understanding the driver for the song you are writing can help frame the process. If I were writing a song for a friend, I would start making notes about that friend, things that are unique to them, how I feel when I am around them, maybe jot down some inside jokes. On the other end, if I am writing a song because I am overwhelmed by an emotion, like feeling lonely from isolation in the pandemic, that might be driven by a very different process of journaling and writing down the feelings and thoughts that I am wrestling with internally.

Once you know why you are writing a song, start playing with the inspiration for it. Create the theme or world around that song. How does it feel? How does it look? If you were to give it a color what would that be? (Don't worry, this has nothing to do with songwriting, it's just a way to get a sense of the full view of your inspiration). You can incorporate imagery, words, feelings, sounds, whatever you need to create the collage around the inspiration you have for this song. It could be something really small or something of worldwide importance. For example, I wrote an entire song about my phone auto-correcting my name and the unfortunate incident that arose from that snafu. It's still one of my favorite songs, called *Sincerely, Treachery*. It was a small, probably insignificant event, but it created a lasting memory and a fun song.

You now have a basic idea, so what do you do? Well, if you are like me and have a terrible memory you need to WRITE YOUR IDEA DOWN. I can't even count (like I said, bad memory) how many times I have had a song inspiration at an unfortunate moment and said to myself "I will remember that one". Then 15 minutes later it's gone, moved on to someone else's inspiration pond. Ways to avoid this:

1. Carry a pad of paper. If you are old

school, then try having paper and a writing utensil everywhere you go. This works for me when I travel; I bring a songwriting journal (or any notebook I find around my house) and write as many ideas down as I can.

2. Text yourself. Utilize technology that is with you at all times and write yourself a text. You could use a handy note app too, but for some reason I like to just text myself random song lyrics that come to me. It makes for a very fascinating read when you go back and scroll through your texts. I also like getting the notification of a text shortly after I send it to myself "Oh, someone texted me, I wonder who it is?" (Bad memory...)
3. Send it to someone else. If you have a songwriting friend, try sending them a lyric. I am very grateful for the friends in my life who I can do this with. I can send a half-created line of lyric and will get a reply with ideas on how to finish the sentence or what comes next. This

> is a very advanced songwriting move so make sure you pick the right partner for this. Texting someone something in the middle of the night that could be misconstrued as a love note is a real possibility with this method.

You might think this is all you need to get started, and maybe this is all you need for today. If you are feeling inspired go ahead and start writing! But if you need some more ideas or want to hear about the joy of the ukulele, read on.

Chapter 2

Why the Ukulele?

Why the Ukulele? Well, because it's easy. I'm not saying this to downplay the amazing virtuoso musicians who play incredibly complicated numbers on this tiny instrument. I say this to emphasize that it is portable and approachable.

The ukulele is portable. You could argue that the harmonica would be even better in this regard, and you would be right, but I still haven't figured out how to play the harmonica, so I'm going to stick to the ukulele. Also, honestly, it's pretty hard to sing while playing the harmonica.

When writing music, I am often not at home. Songwriting can be a great distraction and time filler. I have a miniature soprano ukulele with plastic strings that I purchased for $12, and it is my favorite tool for writing. I stick it in my purse or my backpack and take it to the beach, the park, on road trips, or just to sit on my porch and play around with it. I use this instrument to come up with chord progressions and new sounds for future songs. I have my nicer ukuleles for performing (and have named each one based on their personality), but my mini ukulele is by far my most portable tool and is instrumental (see what I did there?) in my songwriting.

As far as instruments go, I find the ukulele one of the easier ones to learn. I have played piano, drums, bass, and guitar, and yet the ukulele feels less intimidating to me. The added bonus of it fitting my small hands is really nice too. Plus, there are many sizes, so if you do not have small hands, you have the option to choose a tenor or even a baritone ukulele.

The other benefit I find with the ukulele is that no matter what I write it tends to sound happy. I find there is a lot of freedom in that. It's like a rose-colored filter for my music. This lets me write down the darkest thoughts and once that high G rings out I feel like sunshine just showered down on me.

I hope you love the ukulele as much as I do. The tips in this book could be used for any instrument, but I was hoping to reach my friends who have fallen in love with this instrument as much as I have. Whether you are playing a soprano, concert, tenor or baritone, find the ukulele that fits you best, give it a name and start strumming!

Chapter 3

Lyrics or Melody First?

Either the lyrics or melody can come first when writing songs and I often flip back and forth depending on when inspiration hits. More often I find myself with lyrics before melody, but there are many songs I have written to a melody which came first.

When lyrics come first it is because I have a concept or a story that I need to tell. I will have a verse or a chorus and while reading and writing the words I will start humming some ideas of how they could sound. At this point

I will record my ramblings and then figure out the chords by listening and matching chords on my ukulele until I find what fits the melody that I came up with. I record these ramblings either on my phone, or if I have figured out the chords, I will put them in a notebook or even on a spare napkin.

When writing this way, I often find the melody will change many times before I feel it is done. I take my time when coming up with the right melody for my words. Is it moody? Is it light and fun? This is why I will often hum the words until something feels like it matches the story that is being told.

When the melody comes first it is much different for me. I often have a few melodies rattling through my brain. I find it harder to write this way because I will add filler words for a melody and then I struggle with replacing them. For example, I might have had a melody that I really loved but I would then make up words that fit the tones instead of make sense in a sentence. Now whenever I play that chorus my mind goes to the filler words and not the lyrics that I eventually wrote which can get pretty awkward when performing live in front of an audience.

I also find that when I have a melody first, I tend to be really picky about the lyrics that go with it. As melodies are more challenging for me to write, when I have one I love, I want to match it with the best set of lyrics possible. Personally, I think my best songs have come about with a melody first, but I also find it harder to write this way.

There are times where I will have a full set of lyrics and a full melody and find that they nicely match. That is the benefit of working on a few songs at a time, you can use a lyric concept that you had built out previously and match it with a melody you have created. Chapters 4 and 5 follow with more detail in creating lyrics and melodies.

Chapter 4

Writing Lyrics

Now let's get into the really fun stuff, writing lyrics. We touched on this in the beginning "Where does the inspiration come from?" Think about the loops that play in your mind. Try writing about one of those to see what develops thematically, poetically, and inspirationally.

After going through some rough times in my life I was advised to write it all down in a journal. I would write the same things over and over, to the point of annoying myself when I went back and read my thoughts. When I decided to start songwriting, I went back through those journals and turned those thoughts into lyrics. Once they found their place in a song, I didn't feel the need to repeat them in my journals anymore. It was a wonderful discovery and although it won't work for all repetitive thoughts, I do recommend trying it out on those emotions that are stuck. Put them in a song and let them fly.

Situations or stories are a great place to create lyrics. Is there a situation you want to write about? Can you paint a picture with your lyrics that transports someone to the scene you are creating? Can you describe a powerful moment you shared with someone, or a friendship moment carved in your memory? Remember that time you rode the bus and someone had a puppy in their backpack? It doesn't have to be an important moment. Just think of it as a story put to lyrics.

Songs don't have to only be about the big things in life, you could write about the everyday and the mundane. Write a song about your favorite breakfast, your choice of lunch, or take that glass of wine and write a song about its hints of tobacco and chocolate with a nose of blackberry (I obviously am not a sophisticated wine label writer).

So now that you have the words, the story and the inspiration, how do you turn it into a song?

Does it have to rhyme?

No, songs don't have to rhyme. They can if that is your preference, or you can find similar sounds that aren't perfect matches, or you can try writing completely free form with no rhyming. Think about your audience. Are you writing just for yourself? Then it really doesn't matter, write what you like. Are you writing for an audience? There is a familiarity to rhyming that some people are accustomed to. Some songwriters rhyme every line, or every other line, or none at all. Try a little bit of each and see what feels right.

Does rhyming every line feel too much like

a limerick? Does rhyming every other line feel like a poem? Does rhyming nothing at all feel like chaos? Try changing it up occasionally so each song doesn't have the same rhyming pattern and see what you like.

What about the beat and syllables?

This is an area that you might find needs more structure than rhyming. If one line has 12 syllables and the next has 6 and you try to say them at the same pace in the song you might feel like you are tripping over yourself. Try to sing the words in your mind when reading them. Do you need to add an extra word to make it flow, or are you ok with holding out a word over a few beats? This can be challenging for some composers. Your syllables don't have to match on each line, but you should attempt to say them out loud while keeping a steady beat and see if it works vocally. There are times where I will elongate some words or shorten and add some slang to get my lines into the beat. Play with this structure and see what works for you.

Now that you have the lyrics and the beat it's time to look at the structure of the song. It used to be common that you would write a song with a verse/chorus/verse/chorus type arrangement. The verse would be unique and the chorus would repeat each time. Sometimes a bridge, or an alternate pattern in the song, can be thrown in to break up the song and add a new element. Or a pre-chorus could be added to elongate the repeating elements of the song. There is nothing wrong with following a set structure, but it is not a requirement. You can start with a basic verse and chorus structure and then branch into playing with new inserts like a bridge. A bridge or insert can change the cadence and chords for a more dramatic effect. Consider adding a departure to your theme by adding a pre-chorus or some turnarounds. (Turnarounds are typically a couple of measures repeated as in a "vamp" or as a way to lead to, or stall, getting to another place.)

If you want to get into more refined song structure, I recommend doing some research about music theory. For your initial entry into songwriting try a few different structures to challenge yourself but don't feel like you must follow any specific pattern right now. Let your creativity take the lead. Invent your own structures.

Chapter 5

Writing Melodies

Now we are getting into the technical stuff. But this isn't a book on music theory so I'm going to keep it really simple. If you do want to learn more about music theory I recommend "*There's No Such Thing as a Mistake*" by Barney McClure. It is comprehensive and understandable.

This book is about making songwriting easy and accessible for anyone so let's talk about how to write a song if you know nothing about the theory behind it. First, play with the chords you know. If you know 4 chords, try playing those 4 chords in different patterns and listen to what sounds good. If you know more chords then it is even better, although most songs will stay in a certain key (wait, this is getting back to music theory, let's move away from that).

If, when you wrote your lyrics, you hummed along and recorded yourself you can try matching chords to what you hummed. This is very imprecise but at this stage, and if you have a good ear, this is one method to start building your melody.

If you have a starting chord, let's say C, and you don't know where to go from there, and you have determined learning music theory isn't going to happen today, try your trusty friend Google. Look up C chord progression and you will get a bunch of different hits. If we are going to continue and ignore theory for now, just play some of the chords that are recommended and see what sounds best to your ear. Depending on the type of music you usually listen to, something will sound familiar. Most of what you will find will be about guitar, but it is all universal when it comes to chord progressions. Learn the chords for ukulele and start writing your song.

Most music that you see on ukulele sites will just be chord symbols with lyrics and there is an assumption you know the melody. Sometimes you will see guitar or uke tablature (inserts that suggest fingering) and rarely you will see full music notation. In my book *Bawdy Ballads and Salty Songs for the Ukulele* there is both notation "lead sheets" (sheets of music showing the notes and the melody) and "chord sheets" with chords written above lyrics only. A lead sheet showing the melody can be used for learning the singing part or if you are going to do any lead picking or adding other instruments. The chord sheets work great when strumming. Assuming you don't want to do full notation of your song right now let's just write down the chords you are playing above your lyrics and create a chord sheet.

If you are writing the melody first and don't have lyrics that is fine too. Write down the chords and record yourself humming the melody that will go with your song. The recordings will come in handy in the future.

Another way I write melodies or find chords for a song is to just start finding random finger positions on the fretboard. I used to teach ukulele and some of my younger students really enjoyed this game I would play where they would close their eyes and I would play a chord and then ask them to play that chord back to me. (I would usually play whatever chord they just learned) And then when it was their turn, they could play any random thing they could on their instrument and try to trick me by making it extra hard. They would come up with all sorts of tricky finger patterns all over the fretboard and I could never actually guess it, but I would try many times until they were delighted that they had stumped me. I found that playing around with all these funny fingerings would lead me to new versions of chords that I didn't play on a regular basis. I would call these my "made-up" chords and would write the fingering down above the lyrics (numerical fretboard fingering). Now, none of these were truly made up as every chord already exists, but they often were chords that I wouldn't hear every day, or they were variants of chords played higher up the instrument.

So, pick up your instrument, "make-up" some chords, play the ones you know, and have some fun. The most important thing is just give it a try!

Chapter 6

What Now?

You have started writing some music and are wondering what to do with this newfound hobby. You can do whatever you want with it! You can keep it to yourself or share it with others, there really is no requirement.

I had been playing in bands for a while before I started performing my own originals. It was an interesting transition the first time I went on stage and performed something I wrote. I had never felt so vulnerable before, singing about something so personal to a roomful of strangers. What I realized after that experience is that each person experiences music in a different way. Few actually listen to every lyric, and those who do tend to personalize it to something they experienced in their lives versus thinking about why the musician wrote those specific lyrics.

Playing with others made this even more apparent. For a couple of years, I had been playing a song with two other musicians as a fairly regular part of our set list. One time while waiting to go on stage we were talking about what that song meant and all three of us had completely different ideas as to the meaning of the song. And we had all contributed to parts of writing it!

If you are ready to do something new with your songwriting, try a few of these ideas:

1. *Just write for yourself. Keep writing music and don't worry about if anyone else ever hears it.*
   Songwriting is an amazing way to process emotions. You could try writing

songs as an alternative to journaling. Songs can be just for you and there is no requirement to ever share it with anyone else.
I have several songs that I will never publish. Either because they are too personal, too silly, or just really terrible attempts; those ones are just for me.

2. *Play your music for your friends and family and entertain them with your new skills.*
   Make up songs that others might enjoy. When my kids were little I would make up funny songs with their names in them and they were delighted and asked for them over and over again. I have also written very short songs for friends on their birthdays or have played some songs at family gatherings.
   Choose an audience that will support you no matter what and practice your skills on them.
3. *Make videos and post them on social media.*

If you are someone who is savvy with social media and you are happy to be on camera, then give it a go. Display your songwriting skills on your favorite social media channel and put yourself out there. Social media can be a fun way to reach a broad audience and you can take your time getting your video just how you like it. A little different than playing live music.

4. *If you are ready to get out there in the world, start going to some open mic events and perform one of your songs.*
   Open mics are a great way to start meeting other songwriters and work on your performing skills. Find an open mic in a venue that you feel comfortable with and offer up your song. It can be a bit nerve wracking the first time but remember that everyone there is putting themselves in the same position.
5. *Reach out to your local coffee shop and ask if they are open to having performers play.*
   If you want to start playing more than

just one song, start working on putting a set together. See if your local coffee shop will let you play a 30-minute set of your originals. You can ask if you can put out a tip jar and start practicing your skills in public. I played at my local coffee shop when I was getting started and met some great musician friends in the process.

6. *Try busking! (Check with your local ordinances to make sure it is ok to do so, first).*

   If there aren't any open mics or local coffee shops, take your music to the street! Find out if it is legal first, and if so, try playing your music. When playing live music, it is good to know a few covers that people will recognize and then mix in your originals. Don't forget to put out a tip jar.

   Of all the venues I have played, I find busking to be one of the hardest for me. It's why I still try to do it a couple of times a summer to put myself out there and give myself a challenge.

7. *Connect with other songwriters*
   Reach out in your community (social media can be good for this) and see if there are any other songwriters. Do they want to get together sometime? Perhaps do a trade where you each listen to something and provide positive feedback? Put together a group in your community and see if others want to meet for coffee or for a jam session. Find out if others want to put together a small show in your area.
8. *Start a band! There are many websites and online groups to help with connecting you to other band mates.*

It can be really fun to play with others. Start your own ukulele band or find musicians who play other instruments and put together a full band. This can be a fun way to play more music. When starting a band, think about things like how often you want to play, where you will practice, what commitment you are looking for and what types of musicians you want to play with. It's really helpful to set expectations at the beginning and to make sure you vibe well with the other people with whom you perform.

Chapter 7

Inspiration Starters

Now that you have the tools and a framework and know what you are going to do with this, get writing! Have you already started but got stuck? Remember that whatever the first draft is, it doesn't need to be good. Don't wait to find the perfect lyrics or melody, just get started with something.

If you are needing some more inspiration, think about trying some of these topics:

> Firsts – Can you remember your first love? Your first kiss? Firsts can often

bring up emotions that will easily translate into song writing material.

Intense moments – Think of an intense moment and look for that emotion (if you feel comfortable), now write about it. Was there a time of sadness you want to move through? Fear? Elation?

Favorites – Do you have a favorite color? Favorite number? Favorite food? Write an ode to that favorite.

Genre – Try to challenge yourself to write something outside of your go-to genre. Do you always play folk music? Try writing something more heavy metal, or jazz, or try writing a sea shanty!

Gift – Write a song as a gift to someone. Write about a friend for their birthday or anniversary. Write about your favorite teacher. Record yourself singing and playing the song and send it as a gift.

Pets – Look into your dog's eyes and write about their loyalty to you and sing it to them. Write about your cat and their strange way of going about life. Or about your gecko, or weasel, or pet tarantula.

Word challenge – Try writing a song starting with just one word. I like to challenge myself with multisyllabic words. I wrote a song using the word suffocation to see how many multisyllable words I could get into a song.

Irreverence – Try finding something random to write about. I mentioned before about an incident where my phone kept autocorrecting my name to Treachery; I wrote an entire song about it called, "*Sincerely, Treachery*". You could choose an inanimate object, a scene in nature or a funny remark. Write about toast!

You have the tools, the inspiration, and the motivation. Put this book down and start writing your music.

Chapter 8

Music Theory Taster

I have said many times that I would avoid spending too much time on "music theory". By that I meant that for beginners who are just wanting to write some music, the word 'theory' can become a self-imposed hurdle and an excuse to procrastinate.

I have found that books on music theory often leap ahead of most beginners and discourage what I feel are the true tools needed to get started. Music theory can be seen by many as the mathematics of how music is constructed. I do want to state that music theory is actually a valuable aspect of great composing and that there is a place and time in your growth where it will be a factor in taking your creative process to a higher level.

With our four-string ukulele it is important to recognize that nonetheless, it has played a big role in many forms of music. There have been symphonies featuring the ukulele. The ukulele was a factor in the early days of recording jazz, along with the banjo, as both instruments could cut through to the single microphone in the middle of the room much better than a guitar could. Certainly, master ukulele performers have a good grasp of theory.

Here is a very simplistic example of a small aspect of theory that could be an asset to your composing and playing. It is a look at the chords that make the emotional side of composing to fit the mood your composition needs. Here is the simple rule: There are only four kinds of chords, and they are simple to learn.

While many chords have complex color notes

added – especially in classical and jazz – there are only four chords on which they are built.

- Major, minor, diminished, and augmented triads (meaning 3-notes)
- Here is how this can be used in songwriting:
    - Major triad is the "happy" one.
    - Minor triad is the "sad" one.
    - Diminished triad is what is usually used when an actor was tied to the railroad track and the train was coming in old silent movies. Or when the scary and creaky door opens.
    - Augmented triad is the one that often tells of something wonderful coming along, like a flower opening, or a sun rising or setting. It can also help transition one chord to another.

As with everything I have said before, you get to make this work for you, so take these "happy" and "sad" notes and decide what emotion YOU feel when you play them. If these are helpful to start finding the right mood that is great!

It is possible to find these triads in every key. As I mentioned earlier, learn a C chord as a starter. See if you can learn how to change a C chord into one of the four chord types above – then learn and play with these new chords.

I have now shared my tools and philosophy with you. It is my belief that by reading this far, you already have the inspiration and the motivation, now start writing your music! The next few blank pages are the perfect place to start.

A ski bum, sailor and songwriter; Rachel is the swiss army knife of experiences. Born in the back a music store in the small town of Port Townsend, WA to two jazz musicians meant a life of improvisation and adventure was to be expected. She uses her adventurous spirit in her music and songwriting, inviting others to join into the experience of writing their own music.

Printed in the USA
CPSIA information can be obtained
at www.ICGtesting.com
CBHW051741221024
16242CB00036B/910